Authentically You

Finding Yourself Through
Emotion & Connection

UDAY JOSHI

Dear family & friends,

Never be ashamed of yourself, be proud of who you are and don't worry about how others see you. You are enough. I believe in you.

Love,

Uday Joshi

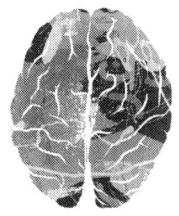

Table of Contents

Preface................................5
Introduction 7

Chapter One: Understanding Our Need
   to Connect...............................13
    What Is a Connection?........................14
    Social Connections Build the Sense
    of Belonging...............................18
    Human Needs: We All Need Connections
    to Thrive 19

Chapter Two: Understanding Our Emotions
   Through Self-Awareness and
   Emotional Intelligence 24
    Emotions and Feelings: Becoming
    More Aware 26

Emotional Intelligence: Controlling Your
Emotions and Reactions (Feelings)............29

Emotional Intelligence Can Only Be
Achieved Through Self-Awareness.............30

How To: Building Self-Awareness and
Emotional Intelligence......................33

Chapter Three: Feeling Down Is an Opportunity
to Get Back Up...............................37

What Is "Purpose"?........................38

Living Intentionally and Authentically..........40

How Can I Become More Intentional?.........43

What If I Don't Believe in Myself?.............45

Embrace Your Inner Leader..................47

Chapter Four: Staying Steady..................52

Boundaries: Saying No *Is* OKAY!............*53*

Gratitude: The Attitude that Keeps on Giving....56

Resilience: The Push Needed to Get Back Up....58

Conclusion....................................63

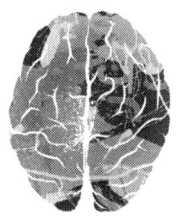

Preface

WHAT ARE YOU MOST GRATEFUL FOR?

Rebecca

I am most grateful for growing up in a loving and caring family that I always can rely on. Even in difficult or stressful times, it calms me down to know that I have a "well-being" place to go to where I receive support, advice and love. I think this helps me to see everything from a healthier perspective and reminds me of what the most important things in life are.

Rebecca was more than happy to be part of the book. She is a fantastic listener, approachable and dependable. Thank you Rebecca!

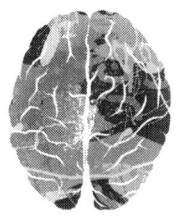

Introduction

When we think about our emotions, we often jump to some that are mostly negative. Perhaps when you think about an emotion, you instantly think "sadness" or "anger". Otherwise, if you are more of an optimist, you may think more positively, thinking of emotions such as "happiness" and "joy". Nevertheless, emotions are much more complex than this: they are intertwined, difficult to understand, and so very curious. They are different from what we understand as "feelings", although the distinction may be difficult to understand – all things we will be discussing throughout this book.

This book is not intended to be a deeply philosophical one, don't worry. Instead, it is one that I am writing to share my view of the world through emotions, namely how our emotions affect every aspect of our being. For example, emotions affect whether or not we choose to apply for certain jobs because we feel like we can't live up to the employer's expectations. They affect whether we feel like we are good enough for a job, for our friends, or for our romantic partners. Our emotions are at the root of everything we experience in life – they dictate whether we appreciate a certain situation or whether we would prefer running away from it as fast as possible.

Throughout my life, I have had my fair share of emotions. I struggled with personal challenges, many of which I discuss throughout this book. For example, now a grown adult, I realize how much of my life as a child has affected how I view the world today. Likewise, I see how young people my age deal with imposter syndrome, or fear rejection, whether it be from an employer, a friend, or in academia. Then, as I grew older, I also learned all about boundaries, namely how crucial they are to our wellbeing and health. Yes, I know, they have become somewhat of a buzzword over the past few years, but they are crucial nonetheless. There is a reason why they have become such a buzzword!

As we will discuss in more detail in the upcoming sections, we currently live in a world that values placing other people before ourselves: we think that we need to be nice to others at all times, and we tend to also believe that if we are *not* nice, the others will find us mean, rude, and hence, will not want to surround us. This perspective, however, is wrong – we need to put boundaries up to ensure that others respect us and our limits.

This book does not solely focus on boundaries, of course. Instead, it looks at all kinds of ways in which emotions dictate the way we live our lives. For example, I will be sharing how overcoming resistance to change and stepping outside my comfort zone was extremely challenging but it was nonetheless crucial for me to find myself and do what I wanted with my life, as opposed to sticking to what I knew and missing out on all kinds of great experiences. We will also be looking at ways in which we hide ourselves, whether it be in your phone (which is what I did), or by socially isolating ourselves, among other ways. Perhaps we feel connected when we use our phones and social media, but chances are that we are giving ourselves the feeling of being connected, all while lacking true connections with people.

Moreover, we will be looking at gratitude – how we can be more authentic, and, live with purpose. That means learning how to recognize that we have things to be grateful for, no matter how much we may think that we do not. Sure, life may be difficult, and we may be going through ups and downs, but we nonetheless still need to realize that there *are* things that are worth being grateful for. The mere fact that you are reading this book means that you have something to be grateful for – you have time and the opportunity to better yourself, and that's an incredible thing to have!

As such, we will also look into being a leader in your own life, including the characteristics of being a leader. When you lead your life with purpose, you do so with certain traits, such as by being an empathetic person, or being a person who knows how to delegate when things are not working out as planned. Then, you also know how to show integrity, and how to communicate with others. Being a leader means leading your *own life* with a tremendous amount of control, and that includes control over how you feel and react – self-awareness and emotional intelligence. Thus, these two concepts will be explored too.

This book is not only about me. It is also about the people who surround me who have helped me become the person I am today. As such, I have also asked friends of mine – people who I am very close to – to share their stories, opinions, and perspectives on the things they are grateful for, what they understand when asked to define happiness, as well as the advice they would give to their younger selves. The goal is to inspire you by learning from them as much as I have, and potentially to inspire you by sharing how I navigated difficult times and self-actualization, too.

Are you ready to learn all about finding yourself through your emotions? When we understand our emotions, we are better able to connect with others – and connecting with others is what keeps us strong. No matter how much you may think that you will be better off alone, do not underestimate the power of being surrounded by incredible people. Every topic discussed throughout this book relates to connection, namely the energy between people when they converse, or as Brené Brown explains it, when people "feel seen". At heart, we are very social people. We *want* to fit in. We *want* to have a group of people that makes us feel like we are part of them. We *want* to belong, simply because our survival depends on it. So, we need to understand where these emotions are rooted and how to leverage them to our benefit so we can truly learn to understand ourselves and find our way.

WHAT IS YOUR DEFINITION OF HAPPINESS?

Simon

It's the small things in life. From having a cup of coffee in the morning to enjoy the moments with the people around me. I live for the present.

Simon, thank you for your trust, you not only have an easy going nature but you inspire myself and others on drawing boundaries, keeping well-being top of mind.

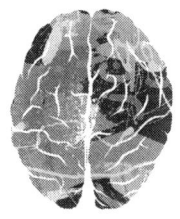

CHAPTER ONE

Understanding Our Need to Connect

First and foremost, let's establish the following: in order to find ourselves, we need to know where we stand within the realm of life. Yes, that sounds philosophical, and no, it's not that complicated. Where we stand is where we are within society – the group we belong to, who we associate ourselves with, whom we relate to, and so on. Human beings are social beings. They want to connect, feel connected to others, and want to know that others appreciate them too. They want to feel like they belong because back centuries and thousands of years ago, this belonging allowed them to survive – having a strong network of social connections kept them from being eaten by a tiger, because John, their friend, would take up the night shift and look out for wild animals. Of course, this is simplified, but you get the jist of it. The moral of the story is that we *want to connect with other people!* We *want* to feel seen, understood, and want others to respect us and *want* us for who we are. And yet, we also live in a society that tells us very often that "we shouldn't care about what people think about us". In reality, this is not possible – we will *always* care about what others have to say about us, no matter what it may be. This is simply because of our wish to survive. So, our connections to others, and whether we feel like we belong, is at the root of all this - how we feel about ourselves, whether we feel like we are in the right place - and hence, needs to be explored in more depth.

What Is a Connection?

Connecting to others is important to our sense of well-being. Our interaction with others has a strong impact on the energy we feel in a relationship. Most of us will learn throughout our various interactions that to make sure we're connecting with others, we need to ask questions about their lives and make sure we're paying attention to their body language and facial expressions. By doing so, we can ensure that we're truly present in the moment and avoid mindless distractions. However, connections, and connecting with others, is more complicated than this.

Connection is a feeling of belonging that occurs when we share experiences and interact with others. This feeling is strengthened when we feel heard, seen, and understood. This bond is important for our physical and emotional well-being. It also facilitates the development of interpersonal relationships – when we feel seen, heard, and understood, we want to forge connections with more people and deepen the ones we already have.

Being connected requires us to be fully present, in the moment. Human connection isn't always easy, and it's not always comfortable – we can end up in situations where we just want to get out of a conversation while also knowing that the very conversation we are in would need to deepen later on (think about your bosses, colleagues, partners, clients, etc). While it sounds like all rainbows and butterflies, some close relationships are messy, and we're bound to make mistakes and disappoint one another. However, this does not mean that something is wrong or that a relationship is unworthy – connections are not always perfect, they take work and effort.

Human beings rely on synchronous moments to connect. These moments are important in our early development and are sought out throughout our lives. For example, dancing and singing together are embodied forms of connection. These activities release endorphins that enhance our connection. Laughing together also helps us feel connected because we share a sense of humor.

Studies have shown that social connections have a significant impact on our health, both physically and mentally. A review[1] of 148 studies found that individuals with stronger social relationships had a 50% higher survival rate. This was true no matter what the person's age, sex, or initial health status was. These findings were also consistent regardless of the cause of death.

Healthy relationships also improve a person's self-esteem. When we know that others accept us, we feel good about ourselves. Feeling like we belong makes us feel good about our capacity to engage in social interaction and, on the greater scale, in our lives. Developing a solid social network of friends, family, and colleagues can help us feel more secure in life. A lack of social support, on the other hand, can make it difficult to cope with stress and mental health. This social connection can be particularly beneficial for those with disabilities, which can be both empowering to those wanting to learn more and with others who are going through similar challenges.

Likewise, such connections are important between people from uncommon backgrounds, or from minority

---

[1] Social relationships and mortality risk: a meta-analytic review by Julianne Holt-Lunstad, Timothy B Smith, and J Bradley Layton

backgrounds. For example, as a third culture kid – a term that refers to children or people in general who grew up in many parts of the world and hence have no true sense of "home," but rather a general sense of many homes throughout the world – can struggle to find like-minded people. They may struggle to create long-lasting bonds simply because they are used to moving around and jumping from one country to the next. In fact, this is something I greatly associate with – as a third culture kid myself, building connections was quite difficult. However, I was a different "third culture kid" – I was the child of grandparents and parents who moved around a lot, so my sense of home was different. They moved from India to Kenya to London – three very different kinds of lifestyles. In my adult life, this is something I had to work on by meeting other people from this same background. When you live in a big city like London, it is possible, but it still leaves a trace as you grow up! Somehow, you know that while you may be making connections with people, chances are that you will not have strong connections to them forever because of the frequency at which you move. However, it is possible nonetheless. Personally, I found people that had many commonalities and shared interests, and it also helps you forge strong relationships with family members as they are the ones who tend to move with you.

....

Social Connections Build the Sense of Belonging

When you're surrounded by people who like you, want to speak to you, and with whom you can have a great time, you feel like you "fit in".

There is a more scientific way of describing this, namely one that was introduced by Maslow in his hierarchy of human needs, which we will be discussing further. As mentioned, having social connections is vital for our sense of well-being and to our overall health. These relationships can be made with friends and family, in clubs and organizations, at work, in school, and in a religious community among others. The need to belong to a group is a natural human tendency. It helps us feel accepted by others, and it helps us strengthen our resilience. However, being part of a group is not easy, and there are many factors that go into determining whether you feel connected to a group – if you feel like you need to put your values aside, for example, you may struggle to feel connected.

Human Needs: We All Need Connections to Thrive

Maslow's hierarchy of needs outlines our basic human needs. These include the physiological needs, safety needs, and needs for love and belonging, among others. Knowing these basic needs helps us understand how to improve our lives – when the needs at the bottom of the pyramid are left unfulfilled, we cannot fulfil the ones at the top. Thus, in order to achieve happiness and self-fulfillment, we must meet these basic needs. This is why Maslow divided his hierarchy of needs into five tiers that add to each other: without the basics met, you can't reach the top, which is self-actualization.

The first level in Maslow's hierarchy of needs is the physiological needs, which include the need for food and rest, as well as the need for clothing and shelter. Maslow's theory emphasizes the fact that when one's physiological needs are met, a higher level will naturally emerge. The theory also suggests that some needs are higher than others, and that a person's needs may change as they grow older. In this way, the hierarchy reflects a person's developmental priorities. For instance, once their basic needs are met, infants are primarily concerned with gaining love and affection from their parents as they represent safety, while an adults' version of safety includes living in a country that is not at war, financial security, access to good jobs, and so on.

Another important area of Maslow's work is social interaction. While most animals live solitary lives outside of mating seasons, humans are highly sensitive to social rejection. Rejection triggers the same neural circuits in our brains as physical pain because social rejection, prior to modernity, meant a higher risk of death. Then, self-actualization, or fulfillment, is another need defined by Maslow. Self-actualization is the desire to live up to one's potential. This includes education, skill development, caring for others, and broader goals – and of course, this is our ultimate goal for driving purpose.

Maslow proposed the hierarchy of needs as a method to understand the motivations behind our behavior. Ultimately, he believed that meeting these needs would result in greater happiness and fulfillment. However, critics have questioned Maslow's theory and its ability to understand human behavior – namely its lack of empirical data to back up the claims made. That being said, it remains one of the most widely accepted concepts in human motivation theory and, if you ask me, it is very applicable to the way we live today. After all, without safety and basic needs, social interactions are more difficult to care about. Likewise, without social interactions and connections, it is much more challenging to self-actualize, simply because we lack others' input in our lives, and because we may not feel like we should bother working on ourselves if we have no one to share the journey with.

Take a moment to think about your own needs. Do you feel that they are fulfilled? Do you agree with Maslow's pyramid? Are your basic needs and needs for safety fulfilled? In this day and age, we may still be able to socialize with people even if we are not fully "safe", such as when we are looking for a job, or when we need to move out and struggle to find a place to live in that fits our budget. Nevertheless, the connections we have can help us here: they can offer comfort and support when we are stressed about such events. Take some time to think about how the connections you have with others have helped you be more in touch with your emotions. Can you speak to others about your struggles? Can you let others challenge you, or do you get defensive when people question your actions or beliefs? These are all connected to your sense of fulfillment – when we feel judged by others, we may be worried about how this will turn out. For example, will they run away if I disagree with them? Will I lose my friends or my partner if I step out of my comfort zone and try to better myself? What if this new version of myself does not fit what they want from me? These are all valid questions, and we can tackle them by better understanding our emotions. This is done through self-awareness and emotional intelligence: the two topics we will be focusing on next.

WHAT IS YOUR DEFINITION OF HAPPINESS?

Catalina

There are different types of happiness with different layers. At a basic level, unattachment to a result or expectation and being in the present. There's simple happiness, for example, when in Luxembourg and there's sun and it makes me feel happy throughout the day or when seeing my cat Mia after a long day of work, not only is there an overflow of love but it gets me back to the present.

Happiness is a feeling of pure detachment and being in the moment. Expectation can hinder that sometimes as with my grandad, where I expected him to be healthy, he has cancer and that made me feel sad in the moment yet so grateful and happy that this was found early.

I can truly rely on Catalina with anything from life to work. She is an amazing accountability partner, best friend, and mentor rolled into one, which is something I'm very grateful for. Thank you so much for sharing Cata!

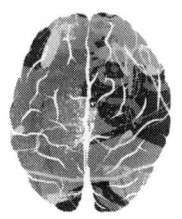

CHAPTER TWO

Understanding Our Emotions Through Self-Awareness and Emotional Intelligence

On one Sunday evening, my nephew and I were watching a Studio Ghibli film called Spirited Away. This is about a 10 year old girl, Chihiro who, while moving to a new neighborhood, enters a different realm to live with the adventure of Japanese folklore spirits and ghosts. Chihiro has a hard time controlling her emotions, which leads to encountering unpleasant and unexpected experiences. She is forced to be responsible for herself, which leads her through experiences of melancholy and eventually belonging.

Being connected to people is one thing, but feeling like we *belong* and like we can openly discuss with them is another.

When we struggle, whether it be at work, university, or within our own personal lives, it can be easier to struggle in silence and on our own. And yet, here is strength in understanding how our emotions affect our actions, and subsequently, in controlling these emotions to then limit how much we let them affect these actions. For example, I tend to self-sabotage. One of the best examples I have of this is when I kept telling myself that I was not good enough, or that I had failed, when I ended up putting weight back on following the pandemic and coming back to the UK after spending time in Dubai on holiday. I let myself feel down for weeks. I allowed my thoughts to take over, and I used negative self-talk in a way that kept me going down this negative path for many weeks. Perhaps you can relate to this? Ultimately, I tackled this by going to therapy to share and embrace my emotions in order to become more aware of how I acted *based* on these emotions. Once you become self-aware, you can take control, and you can actively change how you speak to yourself. This is how you overcome self-sabotage, but it can be applied to any other kind of negative behaviour.

Emotions and Feelings: Becoming More Aware

Understanding your emotions and expressing them in appropriate ways are important parts of self-awareness. It's not easy to do, but there are some key components to learning to express your feelings in healthy ways. First of all, you have to become a good observer of your feelings. Once you are aware of them, you can consider all of your options, and make the best decision. That being said, "emotions" are a concept that many of us use on a daily basis without truly knowing what they are. Let's explore them in greater depth.

Emotions are mental states that are brought on by neurophysiological changes. These changes are associated with thoughts, feelings and behavioural responses, and are expressed as pleasure or displeasure. Generally, we experience feelings and emotions of pleasure or displeasure based on the degree of pain or enjoyment they bring about.

The concept of emotions is complicated. It can encompass a range of different reactions, including those triggered by specific situations, physical changes, and cognitive processes. Historically, academics have attempted to identify the various components of emotion, but these are difficult to establish because of their changing nature – we have emotions all day, every day, and every sociological factor known to man affects these (your gender, your age, what is your occupation, and so on). Each academic discipline has its own definition of emotion and categorizes the various components differently. For example, psychology and philosophy define emotions as mental states and subjective experiences. Sociology, on the other hand, views emotions as a combination of physiological, cognitive, and cultural labels.

For example, if you're watching a horror movie, you may feel nervous and want to hide. Your body responds to fear by increasing your heart rate, dilation of the pupils, and stronger respiration. These bodily changes are triggered by the autonomous nervous system, which triggers these changes before you become conscious of them. While these physical changes don't necessarily reflect feelings, emotions are the driving force behind actions.

Wait, there's a difference between an emotion and a feeling? Indeed. In simple terms, the difference between feelings and emotions is that a feeling is the result of a chemical being released in the brain in response to a trigger. Feelings may be pleasant or unpleasant and range in intensity from mild to strong – it is something that is created when you think about an event, and it may not represent reality. Emotions, however, are conscious

– they happen right there and then. Emotions can also be mixed together to produce secondary emotions. For example, a happy emotion mixed with anticipation creates excitement.

Emotions are reactions to the outside world. For example, if you are still in love with your ex, you will feel excited for them showing up uninvited, or you may also be worried about how you will feel if they do come. This feeling will cause your heart rate to increase, which is the fight or flight response system – that's the emotion. On the other hand, the feeling is the excitement or worry, which is based on the scenario you have created in your head. You are worried because of what could happen, not what IS happening. Your physical reaction shows the emotion, because the reality is that they may come.

Although feelings are generally unconscious, they still influence our behaviors. By learning to understand the difference between feelings and emotions, we can make conscious choices to change our behavior. For example, identifying your emotions and determining the source of your feelings can help you make healthy choices and live a more productive life. If you know that your emotion is X, but your feeling is Y, you can ask yourself why this is the case and reframe the situation so it represents reality.

Emotional Intelligence: Controlling Your Emotions and Reactions (Feelings)

That being said, the distinction between emotions and feelings is not that important to understand to grasp the concept of this book to its full extent. However, learning why you have a certain emotion and how you tend to react is a strong skill to have so you can be in control of your actions. Just like I realized that I was self-sabotaging because I felt bad about having gained weight, I also realized that I was allowing my feelings and thoughts to hold me back from taking action. Once you gain control, you can do anything, including stopping the self-sabotage thinking.

The ability to identify, understand, and control emotions is a vital part of emotional intelligence (EQ, for Emotional Quotient). People who have high levels of emotional intelligence tend to have better mental health and perform better at work – they can respond appropriately to circumstances. They are also perceived as more empathetic and able to lead others. Many employers rate EQ as important as technical skill, and many even conduct EQ tests before hiring employees.

People who are emotionally intelligent understand how to interpret their own feelings and motivate themselves appropriately. These people are also great communicators, and can energize themselves when they are working on new projects. They also understand how to respond to negative emotions in others – for example, they can detach themselves from a person's reaction, namely by understanding that someone else's feeling is not their responsibility. You cannot make someone feel a certain way – their reaction to your actions is theirs. Now, of course, that doesn't mean that you should be an a** to someone for the fun of it, but it means that understanding that you have no control over how they feel about what you do or how they think is truly liberating.

One of the most important aspects of emotional intelligence is motivation. Having a positive attitude will help you avoid being ruled by negative emotions. Positive attitudes can help you deal with stress and other negative emotions – such as feeling bad about how you allowed yourself to gain weight, or missing a few goals that you had in mind towards what you want to achieve. It will also help you feel more optimistic.

Emotional Intelligence Can Only Be Achieved Through Self-Awareness

Self-aware people can identify emotional triggers as they happen and process their emotions before speaking to others. They are more empathetic and open to new ideas and perspectives. They are often more creative entrepreneurs – in the general sense of the term, meaning that you are a solution-seeker – and are less concerned about being Number One in every field, instead focusing on being the best at what they are excellent at. A self-aware person also understands their own strengths and weaknesses and knows when to seek out assistance and when to handle a situation on their own.

Self-awareness can help you be happier and more satisfied with your life. It also helps you better judge situations. You can also make better decisions and have calmer relationships. Being aware of your feelings and thoughts will allow you to make the best use of your gifts and talents. This is essential in today's world because stressful situations are part of everyday life. US President Franklin Roosevelt once said that we are the prisoner of our own minds, and that we can learn to become free at any time – and that starts with understanding how you emote and how to control it.

It is important to understand that emotional self-awareness is not something you achieve in one day. It is a constant process and takes practice. The more you practice, the easier it becomes. This is done through hard work. For example, I grew more self-aware throughout the years. As a child, I was a rather quiet kid and I hid my emotions very often. I did not express my emotions to others, and I did not tell them about my feelings either, neither my friends nor my family. Often, it felt like I was being someone that I was not. As I got older, I decided to go to a meditation retreat called the Art of Living, which helped me get out of my comfort zone and accept the emotions that had built up. Ultimately, I grew more self-aware of these emotions, of the reasons why I was hiding them, and of ways I could stop hiding them. I realized that I could have emotions, and that it was okay.

Self-awareness involves the ability to understand yourself, your thoughts, and your feelings. This awareness paves the way for more effective communication and empathy, which are key for creating meaningful relationships and connections. Self-awareness is a skill, like learning how to play an instrument, and it can be improved over time – just like I did. Perhaps you can go to your own meditation retreat, a therapy session to understand your emotions and thought triggers, or start using a journal if you feel unable to share your emotions with others. Ultimately, you do what you feel comfortable with, and perhaps the more you write, the more you will feel the need to translate these texts into conversations with others.

Self-awareness can indeed enhance confidence in yourself and in others. It also helps develop courage and empathy for yourself, helping you realize that you have strengths and weaknesses, and that you are not any better or worse for them. It is important to understand the different facets of yourself in order to understand how you act and react and, hence, to make the right decisions afterwards. By being more self-aware, I was able to stop self-sabotaging and instead took action. Now, this self-awareness helps me make decisions that work in my favour on a daily basis: I live intentionally.

Self-awareness is essential for making good decisions and managing expectations. Having strong self-awareness can help you set goals and, notice progress. It also helps you balance difficulties with improvements. If you know your strengths, you're more likely to land the job you're applying for, reach the goals you have set, and be motivated to constantly work on bettering yourself.

How To: Building Self-Awareness and Emotional Intelligence

With this in mind, we need to discuss *how* you can build self-awareness and emotional intelligence. To do this, you have a few options. For example, meditation is a great way to do so. As mentioned above, I went on a meditation retreat that forced me to be in touch with my emotions. When everyone around you is there for the same reason, it makes it much easier to let your inner barriers go and to get in touch with how you feel. Another method is to write down your key plans and priorities. When you do so, you become more in touch with what you want to achieve, what your goals are, and what you will do to get to this place. This makes it easier to track progress, to see where you may need help, and to better understand where your strengths and weaknesses lie. You may notice that you cannot achieve all of your goals on your own, and may be frustrated – then, you become self-aware of this frustration, and you can approach the solutions with more empathy for yourself. What can you do differently? How can you solve the problem? Can you ask for help?

Likewise, one of the best ways to find out more about your strengths and weaknesses is to ask the people around you. Ask your friends and family members on the things they think you could improve upon – be careful, you'll need thick skin for this! However, if you tend to get defensive when people criticize you, tell yourself that the people you are asking care about you and want what's best for you. Therefore, they are not saying this in a bad way, but rather in a way that will help you grow as a person.

Otherwise, there are four keys to self-awareness that are well-understood in the community of self-help writers and psychologists alike who support building self-awareness as a tool towards personal fulfillment: changing your context, building skills, thinking differently, and being intentional. Changing your context refers to throwing yourself out of your comfort zone and pushing yourself to be challenged. You will be surprised to see just how much you grow when you are forced to build new skills and learn new things to be successful. Then, building skills is a component on its own – always seek to better yourself, whether this refers to hard or soft skills. Become a more empathetic person, do that online course you have wanted to take for a few years now, and learn how to code if you're interested in this field. Thinking differently will come with time; the more you place yourself in front of new experiences, people, and situations, the more you will face new ways of looking at things, understanding them, and comprehending that there is more than one way to see the world. And finally, live intentionally. Everything you do should be intentional, *authentic*. Do the things you do because you want to do them – not because you think you have to. Pay the bills you need to pay because they allow you to live a life you enjoy, not because you have to. Sure, it may sound ridiculous at first, but *really take a moment to think about it*. Yes, they're annoying to pay. Yes, you wish you could keep that money. And yet, they are what allows you to have a roof over your head, or to be sitting in the café you may be in right now, reading this book.

WHAT ADVICE WOULD YOU GIVE TO YOUR YOUNGER SELF?

Junior

Enjoy the moments and be present. As a kid growing up on a rough estate in London, I never allowed myself to enjoy moments or achievements and just be in the moment. I was always looking forward and planning. Now as an adult I am always striving to be present for my family and friends. I don't want to miss a thing!

ENERGY! It's what I always see in Junior which is awe-inspiring to me. Thank you Junior!

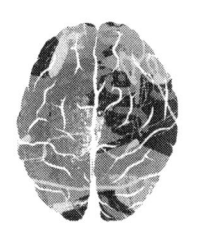

CHAPTER THREE

Feeling Down Is an Opportunity to Get Back Up

When you feel down, or when you feel like you have reached a low in your life, you may feel like nothing is going right. You are just another person going to work or working on your studies, and you don't really know what's next. So, why do you feel down? And most importantly, how can you get back up? In the previous chapter, I briefly mentioned the importance of living authentically and with purpose. This is a true game-changer, so we will be exploring this throughout this chapter.

What Is "Purpose"?

When we feel down, we often feel like there is no purpose behind what we are doing. We are simply doing the same things every day, following the same routine, and getting no thrill out of it. This is where living with intention and with purpose comes in; it shows us that there is something great about life – something to be excited about, no matter what it is. It pushes us to change our perspective to be able to find enjoyment in the smallest things.

But first, let's explore what purpose *is* – because yes, it's more than just a buzzword. Your life purpose is what you came into this world to do. Your purpose guides your behavior, shapes your goals, and gives your life meaning and direction. For some, their life purpose is the home they will build with their family. For others, their life purpose may be their work, which they feel is meaningful. Whatever you choose, you must be consistent and work toward it. To find your purpose, you may want to write down your values and goals. A life purpose statement will help you focus on what you're most passionate about, give you direction, and inspire you to reach new heights. The process for writing your life purpose statement is very personal, so you'll need to take the time to really think about it.

Your life purpose may be something as simple as making something great out of yourself, whatever that may be. For example, if you were the child of a single parent who struggled their entire life to make ends meet, you might want to do something that allows you to be financially free, and free of stress the way they felt it – you may want to get them to this freedom as well. You might promise yourself to make your parent proud every day and make them live an easier life by working hard to give back to them. Or, it could be something as simple as creating a life with your family and feeling fulfilled this way. There are many ways to feel purpose – at the end of the day, it is about what you feel strongly about, and what you want to have accomplished by the time your days on earth are up.

As you dive deeper, you will find an answer that grabs you. It may even make you cry. The best way to find the answer to these questions is to be honest with yourself.

How are you going to save the world?

You can make a difference. Instead of focusing too much on yourself, focus on something much larger.

What you willing to struggle for?

Fulfilment involves effort and trial and error.

What makes you forget to eat?

When are you so immersed in activity that time passes without you realizing.

The more truthful you are, the more likely you are to find your life purpose. And then, once you have it, you can truly start living intentionally.

Living Intentionally and Authentically

Living with purpose can be a powerful experience. It allows you to live with greater determination and happiness. People who live with purpose have clear goals and are concerned with improving their realities so it matches this purpose. This mindset is supported by many great thinkers, who have said that the best way to become fulfilled is to use one's talents and capabilities for the benefit of others, alongside one's own benefit.

In addition to helping people reach their goals, living with purpose allows people to make the world a better place. Through your service to yourself, you become someone that others can look up to. Then, you can share your gifts, and you grow as a person throughout the process. In order to live with purpose, you must first remove any emotional blocks, unhealed wounds, or old patterns that may have impeded your journey. This is done through self-awareness and hard work, as discussed in the previous chapter.

Living with purpose also means having a "why" for living. People with a sense of purpose have lofty goals, are proactive in their pursuit of those goals, and structure their day around the pursuit of those goals. They also spend more time listening to their inner voice. When living with purpose, you will develop an appreciation for the world around you – everything you do contributes to this purpose, from socializing with others because you need it to feel good, to working longer hours so you can enjoy the benefits later on in life.

Living with purpose gives you a sense of meaning and fulfillment. By doing something you love, you will be happier, healthier, and more successful. It will also make you more grateful and resilient in life. It will help you live a life that is truly meaningful to you – you stop seeing yourself as the person who only experiences negative things, to someone who has agency over their fate. Living with purpose is the best way to experience life, and it can help you make the most out of it. Then, we have *intentional living*, which is a "subset" of living with purpose. Intentional living is a lifestyle based on certain values. These values may include religious, political, ethical, or self-improvement ones. Intentional living involves taking a deeper look at how we live our lives.

Ultimately, it is about being more authentic in all areas of our lives.

Intentional living involves asking yourself why you're doing certain things, not just doing them out of habit. It means carefully considering each choice in your life and, if you are not happy with the outcome, knowing that you'll make some changes to get to the desired one. Living intentionally doesn't mean you need to have everything figured out, but it does mean making every decision with a purpose and checking in with your values every day. For example, it means saying no to going out with your friends once in a while if you planned to go to the gym and know you will regret skipping out on it. It also means saying no to your boss if they ask you to stick around until 11 PM if you value family time – this is about setting boundaries, and it's something we will discuss soon.

One great resource for determining your why is "Find Your Why". This book, by Simon Sinek, explores the importance of knowing why we do what we do and what we want. It's written from the perspective of a small business owner, but the principles are applicable to living a life of intentionality. Check it out if you have some time on your hands!

Intentional living means structuring your life around things that make you happy and satisfied. It also means that you don't dwell on mistakes in the past. Consider the circumstances in your life that have triggered negative thoughts or behaviors. How you handled these situations and what you did to respond positively are all important ingredients in intentional living. By doing this, you can create a blueprint of your life and start taking action on it every day.

How Can I Become More Intentional?

Becoming more intentional is not easy. It requires work and may feel awkward at first, but it will lead to healthier patterns. Being intentional doesn't mean getting rid of your belongings, but it does mean learning to make better choices and being more aware of what matters to you. This could mean putting a halt to buying a bunch of stuff that makes you happy now, which is a conditional response that only drains your bank account.

Intentional living involves evaluating your values and goals. You must choose activities and relationships that align with those values. Don't be afraid to set boundaries and say "no" more often. It may feel like a "mean" move, but it's the best thing for everyone involved. Once you know what your values are, the next step is to make sure that you communicate them to others. Then, develop a daily routine that supports your values. Small acts like reading, spiritual practice, breathing exercises, or stretching can help you stay grounded in your beliefs and values. If you can commit to these rituals and daily habits, you can ensure that you're living an intentional life.

Another key aspect of intentional living is setting goals. It will help you identify the parts of your life that don't align with your purpose. A high percentage (96%) of people are living on autopilot (based on a study from Marks & Spencers taken in the UK). Their lives are run by habits and routines that are thoughtless – instead, create routines and habits that fit your greater purpose. Most decisions are made based on what's easiest or most convenient. Intentional living, on the other hand, involves making deliberate decisions that align with your values, and that does not always mean making the easiest choice.

Being authentic is not easy. You may have to go against the crowd to live your life in the way that you want. You may have to make some difficult decisions, including saying goodbye to a relationship in some cases, you might have to let go of a toxic relationship or to a friend who's no longer serving you. However, the more you can be yourself and live in your true light, the more opportunities you will have.

What If I Don't Believe in Myself?

Oof, what a big question! We all go through times where we don't believe in ourselves. In fact, imposter syndrome is one of the biggest challenges that many of us deal with. For example, I have struggled with overcoming resistance to change and being outside of my comfort zone. Changing jobs was a big one, and I dealt with *serious* imposter syndrome. When everything was virtual – during the pandemic – I had to take on a new role and felt like I did not belong there. I felt like everyone around me knew that I didn't belong there. And yet, it was all in my head!

If you're struggling with imposter syndrome, you need to learn to recognize your capabilities. It's important to recognize that no one is perfect, and you need to acknowledge that mistakes are inevitable. You may need to talk to trusted friends and co-workers to get their feedback and see whether this is all in your head – and trust me, it probably is. Hear me out, where you're going is more important than where you came from. Getting feedback from these people will help you realize how good you are at your work.

One way to do so is compatible with intentional living, and it is to live your life like a leader.

WHAT IS YOUR DEFINITION OF HAPPINESS?

Amy

Happiness to me is feeling grounded and present.

We are all guilty of overthinking and all that does is causes anxiety, stress and ultimately makes us unhappy. I deal with that regularly and it's required extra work to minimise.

I've learnt to centre myself and remind myself to look around and enjoy what we have and the small beauties in lift that surround us daily; a friend getting good results, cooking a meal which brings joy or looking out the window and seeing a sunset – these are all the things that make me happy but can't be experienced fully unless I am present in that moment. When I am, no feeling beats it.

Amy is a true kind-hearted, amiable star, and a wonderful support. Grateful to not only be there for her but vice versa. Thank you Amy!

Embrace Your Inner Leader

Being a leader isn't just about leading a big business or being the manager. You need to be the leader of your own life. A leader has specific characteristics that enables them to lead, and they are just as applicable to your personal life, your goals, and your aspiration to live intentionally. There are a number of important characteristics that must be present in a leader. These qualities include integrity, communication, and delegation, among many others. If you want to lead your life well, consider developing these qualities. Once you do, you'll find it easier to motivate yourself to do your best, and you will know that your best is enough (goodbye imposter syndrome!). But what exactly does it take to be a great leader?

Throughout history, people have studied what makes a good leader. A leader is a person who leads or guides – this can refer to almost anything in life. They are the ones who direct people or groups to the right course of action. They are often natural born leaders who take on challenges and make the right decisions for the organization, team, or path that needs to be taken. Some characteristics of a good leader include the ability to motivate people, being competent in their field of expertise, decisiveness, and empathy. However, not all leaders are good and may have certain flaws. Ineffective or incompetent leaders might display traits such as insecurity, quick anger, rudeness, or inconsistency – things that you can avoid through self-awareness.

One of the characteristics of a good leader is their **integrity**. Integrity is about doing the right thing and being accountable for your actions. When things are going well, integrity is a key driver of success. But what happens when things go wrong? Integrity also means learning to admit mistakes and to move on from them. A leader with integrity is also open to feedback. It is important to seek feedback from others who can help you grow. This can help you determine whether or not your approach needs to be tweaked.

A leader can also **delegate** when needed. A successful delegator is able to clearly understand the reasons why a task is being delegated – they know that they can't do everything on their own, and they understand that this does not make them weak or less-worthy of their successes.

The ability to **communicate** is a hallmark of an effective leader. Leaders can effectively communicate through speech, writing, and non-verbal cues. They should match their words and actions to achieve the greatest effect on their audience. These cues build credibility and rapport. In the context we are discussing, this means being able to talk about your successes with others, welcoming their feedback and help, and taking on their critique without allowing it to affect your feelings of self-worth.

Leaders use communication to share their plans, goals, and priorities with their team. They also communicate challenges and barriers to accomplishing the goals. They communicate to teach, inspire, and motivate others to do their best. Effective leaders know when to talk and when to listen. They can also be clear with their ideas and communicate the mission of the organization to different audiences. Again, this is applicable to you: you can inspire others, get their help to overcome challenges, and can share your mission with other people who can help you reach it. You can share your purpose and find like-minded people who will celebrate your wins with you!

Alongside the aforementioned traits, **influence** is also highly present in leaders. The influence of a leader begins with his or her reputation as someone with integrity and strong character. People respect him or her and believe that they know what they're talking about. Leaders must also show concrete results and achieve the desired outcomes – which is why they live intentionally! Their success is sometimes measured by the people they inspire.

Finally, there is **empathy**. The ability to empathize with others is one of the key characteristics of a good leader. Empathy involves understanding the situation of other people without judging them. Additionally, it involves understanding a person's perspective and valuing his or her thoughts and opinions. This characteristic is crucial in leadership, since people will be more likely to want to work with a leader, and help them achieve their goals, if the leader in question truly values the input of others.

An empathetic leader is someone who listens to others without interrupting them while they are talking. This is important because interruptions disrupt the flow of the conversation and can hinder the speaker's ability to share their opinion. An empathetic leader is also willing to put themself in the other person's shoes. In other words, as a leader in your life, you know when to speak about your accomplishments, but you are also there to support others in their own journeys. This is how you surround yourself with like-minded people who want to see you succeed.

Once you are the leader in your life, you can achieve anything.

WHAT ADVICE WOULD YOU GIVE YOUR YOUNGER SELF?

Cecilia

Be more patient and stop thinking about what's next and wanting more responsibility too quickly. Learning to enjoy each stage of life without aiming to burn through.

Cecilia, you are an inspiration. Seeking her guidance has always been of true value. Thank you Ceci!

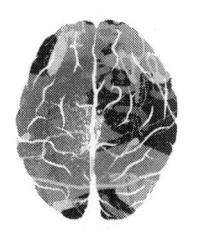

CHAPTER FOUR

Staying Steady

There's great work to be done through progress in order to live intentionally, acting as the leader in your life, and getting past your imposter syndrome. You will still have hard times, and you will continue to be challenged – that's normal! In fact, you should *want* to face challenges! Ultimately, for growth to take place, you need to try new things, face new barriers, overcome some, and then tumble and fall once in a while. Then, you need to get back up. To do this, you need three components:

1. Boundaries – to help you say **no** when you need or *want* to;
2. Gratitude – to have the right mindset to keep going; and
3. Resilience – to get back up when things don't work out as planned.

Boundaries: Saying No *Is* OKAY!

Setting boundaries is an important life skill. The concept of personal boundaries has been made popular by self-help authors and support groups. It involves being clear and open about your values and avoiding compromise when it comes to things that you do not want to compromise on – your core values, the beliefs you have that are unshakable, and so on. By setting boundaries, you protect yourself from being taken advantage of, and you put yourself first.

Setting boundaries is simply communicating your personal values to others. The more you know about yourself, the more you can protect yourself from having your boundaries crossed. Setting personal boundaries is not always easy, but it is worth the effort. It will make your life better and you'll be happier for it. In addition to protecting yourself from compromise, you'll protect your relationships – when people know where you stand, they know that certain things are not okay. Likewise, when you know where you stand, you also know when to step away from relationships that are not in line with your beliefs.

Boundaries depend on a number of factors. For example, boundaries developed by one person are different from the boundaries set by another person. In addition to that, boundaries often change depending on social norms and values. Some people may need to set boundaries only in specific situations while others may need boundaries in every situation. On top of this, many of us don't know our own boundaries! For example, I find it hard to set boundaries with others. In the past, I have said yes many times when I should have said no, and it nearly landed me in burnout. I needed to look at my life from a different perspective and had to view work and life not as a balanced equilibrium, but as something that should be harmonised together. This was just as applicable to the people I met as well, regarding drinking, drug use, and so on. The norms we live in affect how easy or hard it is to set boundaries, but that does not mean that you should not set them. They are there for a reason; they make sure that you respect yourself and, in turn, that others respect you.

To practice self-respect through boundaries, one must understand what is not acceptable behavior. This includes recognizing what makes you comfortable and safe, and what doesn't. You may find it easier to set boundaries with certain people or groups of people whose energy you respect. Likewise, you may be more assertive around other characters or people with stronger energies.

It may feel uncomfortable at first, but it's necessary for the development of self-respect. When we feel good about ourselves, we're less likely to allow other people to take advantage of us. It's also easier to set healthy boundaries when we believe in our own worth. Therefore, it's a vicious cycle – without strong self-worth, we don't have boundaries. Then, without boundaries, we reinforce this lack of self-worth by allowing others to step all over us.

So, learn how to say no. Know what your limits are. Know when you need to take a step back and when you disagree with the way someone is treating you. In order to successfully set boundaries with colleagues, friends, spouses, and, family members, you must first learn to identify your needs. Then, you must prioritize them – remember that you are the only person who will always be there for you, so you need to value that! When you are able to put your personal needs first, you can set appropriate boundaries with others as well. Then, you need to make sure that those around you understand that your needs come first when it comes to your wellbeing. This does not mean that you are being selfish. For example, there is a difference between saying that a boundary is crossed when your friend shows up late every time you meet, and saying that you expect them to always listen to you and never talk about themselves. Use common sense here – and make sure to stay realistic in the process.

Boundaries are an important part of creating a healthy relationship and work environment. They can be set in an effective way by defining them based on core values. Your employer's goal should be to create a healthy work environment where people can work together with respect and cooperation. Setting boundaries at work helps you control your time and space and allows you to focus on what you enjoy outside of work hours. This will help you achieve career advancements, such as a higher salary, a promotion, more responsibility, and more influence later on – this is because people will respect your integrity and ability to prioritize. If your boss does not respect your boundaries, you may need to rethink whether this is the right place for you.

Gratitude: The Attitude that Keeps on Giving

Gratitude is an important part of our well-being. It is the emotion that conveys appreciation and thanksgiving to friends, family, and ourselves. When expressed appropriately, gratitude can be cathartic and help release feelings of guilt or grief. It can also provide a sense of serenity and comfort, something that is very valuable in times of high stress or when you are challenged.

In its broadest sense, gratitude involves recasting negative experiences into a positive light. This in turn produces positive emotions that reduce the pain associated with negative emotions. In addition, it can lead to better decisions and further self improvement.

The act of gratitude is selfless and essentially contagious. By expressing gratitude to others, we show that that they are appreciated and that they are valued - something that affects them positively and fosters a healthy relationship with them. Gratitude also encourages others to reciprocate the gesture. For example, if a friend helps you through a hard time, you're likely want to be there for them in the future.

In addition, to being deeply rewarding, gratitude offers us a powerful space for reflection, renewal, and reconnection. A daily gratitude journal can help you express your gratitude in a variety of ways, and it can be a great way to improve your mental health. Try adding a prompt to your daily journaling to inspire you to write about what makes you grateful. This way, you can look back and see if you've gotten a habit of expressing gratitude. In fact, a great way to introduce more gratitude into your life is to start your day with it. Try this tomorrow: the second you wake up, think about three things that you are grateful for. You can also use an app to help you keep track of your gratitude, and there are plenty of gratitude journal templates on the internet that can help you get inspired.

Resilience: The Push Needed to Get Back Up

And finally, we have resilience. Resilience is defined as the ability of a dynamic system to recover from a setback or adverse event. This ability is also the result of the conscious effort to move forward. Resilience requires the ability to cope with setbacks and hardships, and it is what gets you back up when you fall down.

Resilience can be developed through a variety of strategies, including coping with stress. Although high stress is detrimental to an individual's health and development, there are also positive forms of stress that can promote growth and improve coping skills. It is important to recognize the difference between harmful and positive stress – positive stress could mean anticipation because you are taking on a new, cool project, while negative stress may be the stress you feel when you are on the brink of burnout.

People who have been through difficult times often find it helpful to draw on their experiences as a source of resilience in the present. This can help them to react better to problems that come their way. For example, someone who has experienced a severe illness can draw on their experiences of trauma to help them cope with current challenges. Likewise, if you also went through burnout, you can use it as a way to learn to say no when you have too much on your plate.

Building resilience involves accepting change and being flexible. It can also involve examining your thoughts and feelings to see where they are coming from. This can help you to regain a sense of perspective and a sense of purpose. In the midst of tough times, you can regain your sense of purpose by redirecting your focus and energy to the things that really matter – or by living intentionally. Ultimately, resilience is that little voice in your head that says "come on, you can do it, try again!".

A growth mindset is essential for building a resilient character. Research from Carol Dweck outlines two different mindsets: a fixed mindset and a growth mindset. The former affects how people perceive their abilities and aptitudes, while the latter affects the willingness to work through difficult situations. What you want to adopt is the growth mindset, which is when you choose to learn from your mistakes, as opposed to allowing yourself to fall and not recover. It's simple: whenever a failure takes place, take the time to accept it, learn from it, and move on.

With the right boundaries, a mindset focused on being grateful for what you have in front of you, and the resilience to get back up when you fail, you are all set to find yourself, build the connections that push you further in life, and live every day intentionally.

…………

WHAT ARE YOU MOST GRATEFUL FOR?

Courtney

Gratitude is something that has always been very essential to me and my wellbeing. One of my favorite quotes is "happiness is enjoying what you have, never what you want". It's common in today's society to always be wanting the next best thing, but if you can step back and take a new perspective, you realize you already have so much. Why don't you focus on nurturing what's already growing in your garden instead of trying to always plant something new? Additionally, it doesn't do any good to dwell on what my garden was like in the past, or what it could be in the future. Appreciating it in the present moment is what's important. That's the garden that needs you, and vice versa.

I am overwhelmingly grateful for this life I have been given. I've always been a strong believer of connectedness and fate, and I just know in my gut that I will always be taken care of. I know that I am right where I need to be, when I need to be there. When things go wrong (or *not how I planned), it is always for the better. It always goes better than I could have possibly planned it myself. To me, it's a great relief to trust the process instead of feeling like the burden is all mine. I don't say this to make little of how hard life can be or to say that our actions don't matter, because life is hard, and it does matter how we navigate our behavior in the world. But what we can do is learn what is in our control and what isn't. All I can do is focus on my garden in the present. The rest, the universe will take care of.*

Courtney has had countless experiences which she shares with others and I'm always in awe of her vision and purpose. Thank you for sharing!

....

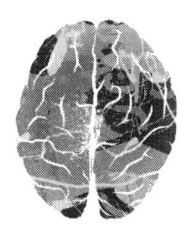

Conclusion

Throughout my life, I have connected with wonderful people from all walks of life. I'm grateful to continue learning from those around me, but also about myself and my emotions. The one thing that led me towards the right place in life was striving for compassion – my communication was nonexistent, yet my empathy was at an all time high.

Living authentically is a balance between representing yourself and breaking away from any defense mechanisms you may have formed since childhood.

Ultimately, I now live with the following vision:

> *"Form a world where happiness and abundance in an individual's life would bring a deed of inspiration and hope".*

I spoke to my friend Sophie on the advice we'd share with others. I admire her for the honest truth she provides and the valuable support she gives herself and others. What Sophie mentions really hits the nail on the head. *Sophie* mentions; *Always remember: you're braver than you believe, stronger than you feel, and smarter than you think.*

Conclusion

WHAT ARE YOU MOST GRATEFUL FOR?

Dominic

I'm grateful for my health more than anything, because without health, we struggle to achieve anything else. Both mental and physical health are at the core of our being, and are at the core of the best versions of ourselves. I am incredibly grateful to have good health at this moment in my life.

Dominic is always growing and sharing his thoughts on what he is most grateful for resonates well. Thank you Dom!

Printed in Great Britain
by Amazon